SCHOOL RULES

Written by Larry Dane Brimner • Illustrated by Christine Tripp

Children's Press®
A Division of Scholastic Inc.
New York • Toronto • London • Auckland • Sydney
Mexico City • New Delhi • Hong Kong
Danbury, Connecticut

For Chippewassee Elementary School
—L.D.B.

For my brother, John Sanders, who is my link to the past,
but is polite enough to keep quiet about it.
—C.T.

Reading Consultants
Linda Cornwell
Literacy Specialist

Katharine A. Kane
Education Consultant
(Retired, San Diego County Office of Education and San Diego State University)

Library of Congress Cataloging-in-Publication Data

Brimner, Larry Dane.
    School rules/ written by Larry Dane Brimner; illustrated by Christine Tripp.
        p.cm.—(Rookie choices)
    Summary: Alex, Three J, Gabby, and their classmates decide on rules of behavior so that
the class can work well together.
    ISBN 0-516-22539-1 (lib. bdg.)   0-516-27389-2 (pbk.)
    [1. Etiquette—Fiction. 2. Behavior—Fiction. 3. Schools—Fiction.] I. Tripp, Christine, ill.
II. Title. III. Series.
    PZ7.B767 Sc2002
    [E]—dc21

                                        2001004945

SCHOLASTIC and associated designs are trademarks and/or registered trademarks of
Scholastic Inc. CHILDREN'S PRESS and ROOKIE CHOICES and all associated
designs are trademarks and/or registered trademarks of Grolier Publishing Company, Inc.
1 2 3 4 5 6 7 8 9 10 R 11 10 09 08 07 06 05 04 03 02

This book is about **manners**.

Mr. Toddle's students were not listening. They were talking and laughing.

Mr. Toddle clapped his hands together. "I think our class is going to need some rules," he said.

Suddenly, everyone got quiet.

The Corner Kids looked at each other. Alex, Three J, and Gabby liked to call themselves the Corner Kids because they lived on corners of the same street.

"What kind of rules?" asked Alex.

"The kind that help us all work together," said Mr. Toddle.

"Like 'No talking'?" asked Three J.

"Talking is fine," said Mr. Toddle. "It's fine at the right time and when we take turns."

Everyone nodded.

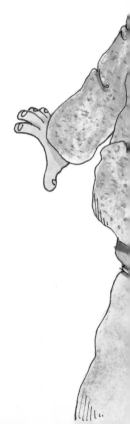

Mr. Toddle passed out some cards. "For homework I want you to think about how we treated each other today. Write down one thing that bothered you. No names, please. Then write down one way to make it better. These will become our rules."

"But if they help us work together, they are like tools," Alex said.

"Exactly," said Mr. Toddle. "Rules are tools for togetherness."

After the bell rang, the Corner Kids were walking down the hall. They were talking about their homework.

Alex said, "Corky Talbot borrowed my new pen without asking. That bothered me because I thought I'd lost it."

"I cut in front of Ben Wong at the pencil sharpener," said Three J. "I should have waited my turn."

Just then a big kid pushed
between them and ran out the door.

"Move it!" he hollered over his
shoulder.

Gabby snapped her fingers together. She took out her card. She described what happened.

Then she wrote, "No pushing. Say 'Excuse me, please,' to get by other people."

Rules
Tools for Togetherness

Problem: Solution:
Somebody Ask
borrowed before
my new borrowing
pen something.
without
asking.

Alex and Three J wrote down their ideas, too.

The next day everyone shared.
Mr. Toddle wrote down what they said.
"These look like some fine rules,"
he said.

Alex raised his hand.
"Tools for togetherness," he said
when Mr. Toddle called on him.

Everyone laughed, even Mr. Toddle.

ABOUT THE AUTHOR

Larry Dane Brimner studied literature and writing at San Diego State University and taught school for twenty years. The author of more than seventy-five books for children, many of them Children's Press titles, he enjoys meeting young readers and writers when he isn't at his computer.

ABOUT THE ILLUSTRATOR

Christine Tripp lives in Ottawa, Canada, with her husband Don; four grown children—Elizabeth, Erin, Emily, and Eric; son-in-law Jason; grandsons Brandon and Kobe; four cats; and one very large, scruffy puppy named Jake.

SPINNINGWHEEL
BIKE SHOP

SCHOOL

COTTONWOOD

COTTONWOOD STREET

LONG STREET